AF228540

HIP-HOP ARTISTS

LIL UZI VERT

EMO RAP **PIONEER**

BY CYNTHIA KENNEDY HENZEL

Essential Library

An Imprint of Abdo Publishing
abdobooks.com

ABDOBOOKS.COM

Published by Abdo Publishing, a division of ABDO, PO Box 398166, Minneapolis, Minnesota 55439. Copyright © 2022 by Abdo Consulting Group, Inc. International copyrights reserved in all countries. No part of this book may be reproduced in any form without written permission from the publisher. Essential Library™ is a trademark and logo of Abdo Publishing.

Printed in the United States of America, North Mankato, Minnesota.
102021
012022

Cover Photo: Scott Garfitt/Shutterstock Images
Interior Photos: Amy Harris/Invision/AP Images, 4; Scott Dudelson/Getty Images Entertainment/Getty Images, 6; Astrid Stawiarz/Getty Images Entertainment/ Getty Images, 9; Matt Sayles/Invision/AP Images, 12–13; Shutterstock Images, 14, 22, 32, 60, 77, 85, 91; Ted Alexander Somerville/Shutterstock Images, 17; M. Moira/ Shutterstock Images, 19; Katy Winn/AP Images, 25; Tommaso Boddi/Getty Images for ASCAP/Getty Images Entertainment/Getty Images, 27; Deborah Lowery/Polaris/ Newscom, 29; Michael A. Walker Jr./Shutterstock Images, 30; Michael Zorn/Invision/ AP Images, 34–35, 41, 88; Paul Morigi/WireImage/Getty Images, 37; Debby Wong/ Shutterstock Images, 38; Wenn Rights Ltd/Alamy, 44–45; Featureflash Photo Agency/Shutterstock Images, 46; Chris Szagola/AP Images, 48; Matt Crossick/ PA Wire/AP Images, 51; Cristian Ghisla/Shutterstock Images, 54; Anthony Behar/ Sipa USA/AP Images, 56; MPI04/MediaPunch/AP Images, 58; John Bazemore/AP Images, 62; Nejron Photo/Shutterstock Images, 63; Daniel DeSlover/Sipa USA/AP Images, 65, 70–71, 96; L. E. Baskow/LeftEye Images/Sipa USA/AP Images, 67, 95; Tami Chappell/AP Images, 73; Jerod Harris/Getty Images for West Coast Cure/Getty Images Entertainment/Getty Images, 75, 80; Zyra Lee Zhang/Shutterstock Images, 82; Sutipond Somnam/Shutterstock Images, 83; Sthanlee B. Mirador/Sipa USA/AP Images, 87; Steven Ferdman/Everett Collection Inc/Alamy, 92

Editor: Arnold Ringstad
Series Designer: Laura Graphenteen

LIBRARY OF CONGRESS CONTROL NUMBER: 2021941118
PUBLISHER'S CATALOGING-IN-PUBLICATION DATA

Names: Henzel, Cynthia Kennedy, author.
Title: Lil Uzi Vert: emo rap pioneer / by Cynthia Kennedy Henzel
Other title: emo rap pioneer
Description: Minneapolis, Minnesota : Abdo Publishing, 2022 | Series: Hip-hop artists | Includes online resources and index.
Identifiers: ISBN 9781532196171 (lib. bdg.) | ISBN 9781098217983 (ebook)
Subjects: LCSH: Lil Uzi Vert (Symere Woods), 1994---Juvenile literature. | Rap musicians--United States--Biography--Juvenile literature. | Rap (Music)-- Juvenile literature. | Lyricists--Biography--Juvenile literature. | Emo (Music)-- Juvenile literature.
Classification: DDC 782.421649--dc23

CONTENTS

CHAPTER ONE
ONE DAY
4

CHAPTER TWO
FAITH
14

CHAPTER THREE
THE REAL UZI
22

CHAPTER FOUR
FIRST ALBUM
34

CHAPTER FIVE
FASHION
46

CHAPTER SIX
IT'S NOT ALL FUN
56

CHAPTER SEVEN
UZI'S BACK
70

CHAPTER EIGHT
UZI'S NEXT MOVES
80

CHAPTER NINE
INFLUENCE AND IMPACT
88

TIMELINE 98
ESSENTIAL FACTS 100
GLOSSARY 102
ADDITIONAL RESOURCES 104

SOURCE NOTES 106
INDEX 110
ABOUT THE AUTHOR 112

WE DIDN'T DO ANITHI
WRONG B
WE DIDN'T ANITHIN
RIGHT
HOME A GLASS
HOME WATCH
SO VERY NICE
SCRATCH
EXCELLENT
THEE
MAKE THEE
ANITHING GOES
GUCI CREW
YOUR LAST

ONE DAY

It was February 2017, and Lil Uzi Vert was on tour in Europe with The Weeknd's *Starboy*: Legend of the Fall world tour. He and The Weeknd, a Canadian singer born Abel Makkonen Tesfaye, had gotten close. The Weeknd was a few years older than Uzi, and Uzi's DJ, PforReal, had encouraged Uzi to learn from the more experienced performer. PforReal, born Paul Huston Jr., was the son of legendary DJ and producer Prince Paul. PforReal had been Uzi's DJ for three years. He knew Uzi had experience performing live, but this was his introduction to the huge crowds of 30,000 or more that flocked to international concert tours.[1] Uzi was learning a lot.

Lil Uzi Vert's release of the song "Money Longer" in 2016 had brought attention to the young artist, and he was a hit on The Weeknd's tour. Uzi was on fire when he was onstage. He had a tremendous amount of energy, jumping and dancing and interacting with fans. He gave his performances everything he had. It was exhilarating.

New releases in 2017 launched Lil Uzi Vert to worldwide fame.

DJ PforReal worked with Lil Uzi Vert from the earliest days of the young rapper's career.

Still, the tours were a grind. Every few weeks there was a new venue, which involved moving equipment, doing rehearsals on a new stage, figuring out the sound checks, and settling into a new hotel. Plus, singing and moving as Uzi did onstage tired him out by the end of a set. In their off time, Uzi and other performers on the tour would wander the new cities they visited. But often it felt good just to go back to the hotel for some downtime.

ON A WHIM

One evening in Switzerland, Uzi decided on a whim to upload a few new songs to SoundCloud. SoundCloud was the streaming platform he used to release his music to the world. In Geneva, Uzi had lost two phones containing the only copies of some of his unreleased songs when he had dived into a crowd of fans. It was a painful loss. Still, he had hundreds of other songs that had not been released.

Uzi borrowed PforReal's laptop and began scrolling through some of the unreleased songs. Finally, he chose four of them. He had no idea that his choice was about to change his life. He didn't even tell anyone what he was putting out.

A QUICK FIX

One of the songs he chose had an unusual history. His producer, TM88, had lost the original track in a bizarre situation at an airport in Florida. While the producer was waiting to board a plane back to

Atlanta, Georgia, where he was based, the airport was attacked by a mass shooter. Five people were killed. As screaming crowds fled, TM88 dropped his laptop charger.

When TM88 got back to Atlanta, he couldn't connect his laptop to his studio equipment. He didn't have access to his saved beats, but he had ideas swirling in his head, so he quickly used other gear to record more beats. TM88 decided to send one of these beats, a revised version of one he had worked on years before, to Uzi. He worked on a laptop with a cracked screen. After reviewing the planned track, he decided the song needed a faster beat. He changed the tempo, reworked the song, and sent it off to Uzi.

Uzi decided that this new version of the song would be one of the four he uploaded to SoundCloud on February 26, 2017. The song just needed a title. Uzi named

TM88

TM88, whose real name is Bryan Simmons, is a producer and DJ from Atlanta. He is a member of the record production and songwriting team 808 Mafia. TM88 is known for his drum-heavy beats for hip-hop and rap stars such as Lil Uzi Vert, Future, and Travis Scott. Lil Uzi Vert and TM88 have worked together on many projects over the years, including TM88's 2019 song "Slayerr."

it "XO Tour Llif3," pronounced XO Tour Life. The title was an homage to The Weeknd, who had founded the record label XO.

BRITTANY BYRD

Brittany Byrd was Lil Uzi Vert's girlfriend from 2014 until the summer of 2016. She is a stylist and designer. Originally from Los Angeles, Byrd moved to New York to attend Parsons School of Design. Known for her unique style, she was inspired at an early age by Japanese youth culture and anime. Her pink hair was inspired by the pink merchandise from Hello Kitty. When asked about what brought her and Lil Uzi Vert together, she explains that it was "knowing we are both not of this planet. . . . Two aliens in America."[4]

It was a different kind of song compared with most rap releases at the time. "XO Tour Llif3" evoked the feelings of young heartbreak. Uzi and his girlfriend of three years, designer Brittany Byrd, had broken up the previous summer. The song also involved dark themes, including suicide and drugs.

THE UNBELIEVABLE

"XO Tour Llif3" got one million plays in the 24 hours following its release.[2] By the time the group got to London, England, and Uzi played a show at the Electric Ballroom on

March 6, the fans knew all the words. He sang the track onstage in London while opening for The Weeknd's tour, then released it as a single on March 24.

Lil Uzi Vert released his first studio album, *Luv Is Rage 2*, on August 25, 2017. It included "XO Tour Llif3." The album debuted at Number 1 on the *Billboard* 200 in its first week. The song was Uzi's first top-ten single, reaching Number 7. "XO Tour Llif3" won Song of the Summer at the 2017 MTV Video Music Awards. Praising the song, Joe Coscarelli of the *New York Times* wrote, "It doesn't get better."[5] Eventually, the track would go seven times platinum.

Back in New York, "XO Tour Llif3" got another boost. Uzi sang the song as he danced with some of his one-of-a-kind moves, notably the shoulder shimmy—a slow one-shoulder roll often

MIXTAPE VS. ALBUM

Mixtapes and albums are both compilations of songs. But there are differences between the two types of releases. Mixtapes are uploaded online and are often free to download, while albums are more formal projects released for sale. The main difference is the goal of the project. Mixtapes offer exposure to new artists. They can be produced and uploaded by the artist, though they are sometimes released by record companies too. Their success is judged by how many downloads they receive. The goal of an album, which is professionally produced, is to earn critical acclaim and make money.

accompanied by an eye roll. A challenge went out encouraging fans to upload their own version of the Uzi move while dancing to the song. The #LilUziVertChallenge went viral. Lil Uzi Vert was famous around the world, and he was just 23. He had come a long way from being an average North Philly high school kid.

"Channeling the goth-tinged emotion of some of his favorite rockers, including Marilyn Manson, the Philadelphia rapper turns a morbid hook–'Push me to the edge/ All my friends are dead'–into a delirious sing-along."[6]

–Kristin Corry, *Pitchfork*

Chapter TWO

FAITH

Symere Bysil Woods watched his friend William Aston freestyle rapping to an instrumental by Chris Brown. The other kids at Northeast High School in Philadelphia, Pennsylvania, went wild. Symere felt a little jealous over all the attention William was getting. Symere played the trumpet in the high school band—mostly for an easy grade—but had never tried rapping.

Symere spent a lot of time at home listening to rock and hip-hop. His father had introduced him to Philadelphia rap artists like Beanie Sigel, a member of the rap group State Property. He also listened to rock bands like Paramore and the All-American Rejects. In a departure from most kids his age, Symere was a huge fan of controversial metal artist Marilyn Manson. He had fallen hard for Manson's music, downloading everything he could find.

Other than his taste in music, Symere was a typical North Philly high school kid. He liked skateboarding, playing basketball, and hanging with his friends. Symere

Lil Uzi Vert grew up in Philadelphia and had his first experience with rapping there.

was born on July 31, 1994, in the Francisville area of Philadelphia. His parents had split up when he was young, so he lived alternate weeks with his mother and father. Symere was small, standing about five feet four (163 cm). He was bullied in high school and started listening to rappers Wiz Khalifa and Meek Mill, who was his favorite of all time.

Symere was so jealous of William's success that he went home and started practicing rapping over beats he found on YouTube. He told William he could rap, and William pressed him to show what he could do. Finally, Symere went to the studio with his friend and tried it out. William was impressed. The two were soon working together.

Meek Mill was one of Symere's rap idols in high school.

STEAKTOWN

In 2010, when Symere was in tenth grade, he teamed up with William and another friend, named A.Y., to form their own group, Steaktown. The name may have been a nod to their city's famous sandwiches, Philly cheesesteaks. Symere

"I really didn't want to rap; I was just a regular kid. My friend—his name is William Aston—we went to the same high school together, and he was rapping. He put out a freestyle over Chris Brown's 'Look at Me Now,' and it was fire, and the whole school went crazy."[1]

—Lil Uzi Vert

began performing with the name Sealab Vertical, then changed it to Steaktown Vertical. He used the word *vertical* as a metaphor for shooting to the top. The name was usually shortened to Vert. Soon, Symere adopted the rest of his stage name, Lil Uzi. *Uzi* refers to a famous model of automatic weapon. The name came from a comment a SoundCloud listener made about his rapid delivery of lyrics—the words came as fast as shots from a machine gun.

The group had some success. In 2012, it released a locally popular track called "Steaktown Anthem." In the music video, Symere is seen walking shirtless through an alley with his friends and rapping while sitting on top of a basketball rim.

Symere began to think he might have found something he was really good at. The songs he put on SoundCloud first got a few dozen hits, then a few hundred. It was hard for him to believe it when the numbers started growing even larger.

The name *Uzi* comes from the Uzi submachine gun, a model that originated in Israel in the 1950s and has since been exported widely around the world.

THE GROUP BREAKS UP

When Uzi was 17, the musical group broke up. Shortly after that, he dropped out of high school. Following his mother's insistence that he get a job, he went to work at a supermarket called Bottom Dollar. He lasted there only four days. Being a rapper had more appeal than retail work. His mother, unhappy with him dropping out of high school and then quitting a job, kicked him out of the house. She wasn't a fan of his decision to pursue a career as a rapper.

Uzi moved in with his grandmother. She was living in a nursing home at the time, so there wasn't much room. Still, Uzi and his grandmother had always been close, and he didn't mind the cramped quarters. She encouraged him to work at his music. She even bought him his first set of grills. These are decorative covers, often containing gold, silver, or inlaid jewels, that snap over the front teeth and are popular in hip-hop culture.

Now the question was whether he could actually make a living as a rapper. He got a face tattoo, his first of many tattoos and piercings. The tattoo was the word *FAITH* inked just above his hairline. He chose the word as a reminder to himself. If he wanted to succeed, he believed he needed to have faith in himself.

"I just want to be successful. I'm not going to sit here and be like, 'I want to win a Grammy' or whatever; if that comes, that's awesome. But I just want to be successful and provide for my whole family and get my family out the hood."[2]

–Lil Uzi Vert

SOUNDCLOUD
15:18
Find music you love.
Discover new artists.
Create an account
Sign in

THE REAL UZI

Lil Uzi Vert went to work to achieve his dream of being a star. He uploaded songs on SoundCloud, and it wasn't long before his work got the attention of Philadelphia music producer DJ BuzzWorthy. BuzzWorthy introduced him to producer Charlie Heat and DJ Diamond Kuts, the top DJ for Philadelphia hip-hop radio station Power 99. Uzi found that knowing the right people and learning from their expertise would help propel him upward.

Uzi worked with several producers, including SpaceGhostPurrp and Charlie Heat, who would become a regular collaborator. Uzi uploaded the resulting songs on SoundCloud, where they got a few hundred and then a few thousand plays. That seemed like a lot at the time, and the response inspired Uzi to keep working.

On January 19, 2014, Uzi released his first major project, *Purple Thoughtz Vol. 1*, at the age of 19. It was an eight-song mixtape. One of the singles, "White S—," produced by SpaceGhostPurrp, got a lot of attention. It would eventually go viral in 2017.

In the early days of his career, Lil Uzi Vert was able to use SoundCloud to connect directly to his fans without having to go through a traditional record label.

Uzi moved on to his next project, working with Charlie Heat on the song "Uzi." His work was becoming more professional, and DJ Diamond Kuts played the song on the radio. The song introduced him to a whole new group of professionals willing to work with him.

DJ DIAMOND KUTS

Diamond Kuts, born Tina Dunham, is a Philadelphia native. She is the first female DJ to have a slot on Philadelphia radio station Power 99. Dunham liked music as a kid. When her father gave her a DJ kit for Christmas one year, she knew what she wanted to do. She practiced at home and began dropping mixtapes of her work. She finally got a gig DJing at a local store in Philadelphia that sold sneakers. Kuts was hired by Power 99, beginning with a slot on Saturday morning before dawn. She was soon moved up to more prime slots and has toured as a DJ for the rapper Lil Mama.

LEARNING THE BUSINESS

One of the people who heard "Uzi" on the radio was Don Cannon, who heard Uzi's music in the car while driving around Philadelphia. Cannon worked for Def Jam Recordings, a record label that focused on hip-hop and was owned by Universal Music Group. He was in the artists and repertoire (A&R) department. A record company's A&R staff is responsible for finding and developing new talent.

DON CANNON

Don Cannon was born in Philadelphia in 1979. He has been a successful DJ, musician, and executive in the music industry. In 2005 Cannon produced *Let's Get It: Thug Motivation 101* by Young Jeezy. He became Vice President of A&R at Def Jam in 2012 and was named by hip-hop magazine *XXL* as one of the 30 best hip-hop producers of 2016. Cannon produced and cowrote six of the songs from Uzi's 2017 *Luv Is Rage 2* album.

Cannon signed Uzi to The Academy imprint at Def Jam. The Academy's DJs and other production specialists were dedicated to helping new artists find commercial success. Cannon then produced Uzi's first professional mixtape, *The Real Uzi*. The tape was released on August 5, 2014. It had been just two years since his high school release of "Steaktown Anthem."

After *The Real Uzi* was released, Uzi signed a record deal with Atlantic Records under the Generation Now imprint, which was run by Cannon, DJ Drama, and Leighton Morrison. On October 20, 2015, he released his first mixtape with Generation Now, *Luv Is Rage*. It included appearances from Wiz Khalifa and Young Thug. Young Thug would become a good friend to Uzi. The mixtape got fairly positive reviews. Darryl Robertson of *Vibe* called the project "solid."[1] HotNewHipHop declared him one of the "breakout artists of 2015," but it also noted, "He's still

In addition to his work as a record executive, Don Cannon has produced tracks for a variety of major artists.

got a ways to go in terms of tightening up his sound and forming a distinct identity."[2]

In April of the next year, Uzi released his second mixtape, *Lil Uzi Vert vs. The World*. This project debuted at Number 37 on the *Billboard* 200 and eventually went platinum. One of the songs on this mixtape, "Money

Longer," made it onto the charts. Uzi had reached the big time, and in "Money Longer" he cataloged his success with lyrics that detailed how he was making more money and getting faster cars. Uzi's luxurious lifestyle was a theme that would continue in his later work.

On July 31, 2016, he released another mixtape, *The Perfect LUV Tape*. He had earned a spot as one of the 2016 *XXL* Freshmen, a recognition for rising rap artists in their first year. He used the SoundCloud platform to release new types of music, trying to avoid being pigeonholed into one genre. The song "Do What I Want" on

The Perfect LUV Tape is a tribute to his growing confidence. By 2016 he was SoundCloud's most followed artist. Although he was not sure whether he totally liked the idea, he also realized that music and fame were now his life.

Uzi performed at the Roots Picnic music festival in October 2016.

FIRST NUMBER 1

In addition to helping him become more professional in his own music, working with Generation Now gave Uzi opportunities to work with other artists that the imprint represented. After *The Perfect LUV Tape*, he did a collaboration with Gucci Mane. Mane, born in 1980, was an established rapper who was a pioneer of trap music in the 1990s. The album that Gucci and Uzi did together, *1017 vs. the World*, got lukewarm reviews. Putting Uzi and Gucci

Uzi's collaboration with Gucci Mane didn't pan out critically.

together tended to emphasize the distance between the traditional trap of the older Gucci and the manic world of Uzi.

Another collaboration was a big success. Uzi was the featured vocalist in the 2016 song "Bad and Boujee" by Migos, boasting of his wealth and high-end lifestyle. The song got a slow start, but by December it was spawning internet memes, with users rhyming the refrain "rain drop, drop top" in creative ways.[4] During Donald Glover's acceptance speech at the 2017 Golden Globes, he mentioned the song, giving it even more attention.

"Bad and Boujee" jumped to the top. It became the first *Billboard* Number 1 single for both Migos and Lil Uzi Vert when it peaked in that position in the week of January 21, 2017. It was streamed more than 500 million times in its first two years.[5] At the Billboard

The collaboration between Lil Uzi Vert and hip-hop trio Migos turned out to be a smash hit.

Music Awards, the song was nominated for Top Rap Song and Top Rap Collaboration. In addition, Lil Uzi Vert received a nomination as the Top New Artist. The song also got a nod from the 60th Annual Grammy Awards by being nominated for Best Rap Performance. Uzi himself was nominated for Best New Artist at the Grammys.

Although Lil Uzi Vert did not win the Grammy Awards, the recognition showed that he was moving up in the industry. Still, he seemed to take his rising fame day by day. In response to what he would be doing next after his Grammy nominations, Uzi shrugged and said, "Waking up. Eating some Pop Tarts."[6]

"I ain't stopped raging since I got here. I haven't stopped. I'm raging right now. I might seem calm, but under these glasses I'm raging. Always. I don't stop raging. I don't stop at all."[7]

–Lil Uzi Vert

FIRST ALBUM

Cannon went to work with his new talent. They began production on the project *Luv Is Rage 2*, which would be Lil Uzi Vert's first professional album. Cannon pulled in sound engineer Kesha Lee to work with them. Cannon, Lee, and Uzi would form the core of the production team.

They began work in December 2016 and took a trip to Hawaii in early 2017 to concentrate on recording the album. The team spent two and a half weeks in Hawaii, then came back and worked on the album until Lee finally finished in August. It was a grueling schedule, involving work every day except when Uzi was performing somewhere onstage.

The first thing they had to do was find the beats. People emailed Uzi beats he might like, and Lee asked for beats to be sent to her. At times, Cannon created some beats himself. Uzi would listen to a beat for a short while, then go into the sound booth to record. He liked spontaneity—he didn't want to spend too much time rehearsing. As they worked, Uzi constantly discovered

Energetic performances and fresh new songs pushed Uzi's career to new heights.

new and better elements to incorporate. Uzi released the extended play (EP) *Luv Is Rage 1.5* in late February 2017 as a teaser for the coming album.

Uzi was a perfectionist, and he knew he would have just one shot at his first album. He even did some of his own drops, moments in the tracks where the music stopped and he would keep singing. He could mute the music himself, and when he turned the sound back on he would be right on the beat. If anything was slightly off, Lee would clean it up. The only instrument Lee recorded for the album was an electric guitar for "The Way Life Goes." Two other rappers contributed

As a sound engineer, Kesha Lee helped shape Cannon's beats and Uzi's raps into a smooth, polished album.

to the album. Pharrell Williams recorded his part in Los Angeles when the team stopped there on the way back from Hawaii. The Weeknd sent in his contribution.

Once the recording was done, Lee did the mixing for the album. This is where adjustments are made to volume; vocals, beats, and instruments are balanced; and changes are made that emphasize certain parts of the song or eliminate parts that are distractions. The various elements

The Weeknd has worked with Uzi multiple times, touring with the rapper and appearing on his first album.

of the song are made to work seamlessly together. Once the album was mixed, Lee did the mastering, a process that ensures the music's quality comes across properly no matter what format it is released in. This included finalizing the transitions between the songs to make them all work together.

Lil Uzi Vert released *Luv Is Rage 2* on August 25, 2017. It featured his breakout song "XO Tour Llif3." The album

debuted at Number 1 on the *Billboard* Hot 100, and it
would eventually go platinum. By the time Uzi returned
from his next tour, he had more than one billion Spotify
streams. He received
recognition from the MTV
Video Music Awards and
from the Grammy Awards.
He appeared on the cover
of *Billboard* magazine for
December 30, 2017, and
in the Fall 2017 edition of
XXL magazine.

    The praise he
appreciated the most
may have been from
his high school hero
Marilyn Manson. Manson
praised Lil Uzi Vert for his
authenticity, saying, "Real
scars show. Mental, physical, musical, all of them."[1] He also
encouraged Uzi to move ahead to do the rock album he
had in mind, saying that Uzi could invent a whole new
sound in rock.

EVOLUTION OF STREAMING

Streaming platforms such as Spotify and Apple Music have come a long way since the early days of digital music. They now feature high-quality audio and broad music libraries. Some platforms can show the lyrics so that listeners can sing along with their favorite songs. Music streaming has become so popular that the Recording Industry Association of America today uses music streaming figures in calculating an album's sales benchmarks.

SHOWMAN

Beginning in the summer of 2015, Uzi had been introduced to the world of large-scale live performances. In addition to recording music, DJ Drama took him on tour for Fall Out Boy and Wiz Khalifa's Boys of Zummer concert tour. Uzi had performed live to smaller audiences. Drama was eager to see how the young rapper performed with larger crowds, and Uzi didn't disappoint. When Uzi got onstage to sing Carnage's single "WDYW," the crowd went wild.

The Boys of Zummer performers played to crowds of 15,000 to 20,000 fans each night.[2] For Uzi, it was a high he could hardly imagine.

KESHA LEE

Kesha Lee was born in Alabama in 1989. She got a job at a radio station editing commercials, and she liked working with audio so much that she took an 11-month audio engineering course at the Atlantic Institute of Music. The Atlantic music scene was very welcoming, and she got to know a lot of musicians and other techs. Lee says that being a woman in a male-dominated industry has been challenging. She sometimes has to remind people that she knows what she is doing—they just need to tell her their end goal, and they don't need to explain how to do every step she needs to take to get there.

Once he had been part of the crowds at concerts put on by his favorite performers. Now he was onstage.

Uzi dashed past the huge crowd toward the stage for a late 2016 show in Philadelphia.

Uzi's appeal on the concert stage came from his huge amount of energy and charisma. He would jump, dance, and often join the crowd and interact with fans. He just seemed to be having a good time, and everyone around him wanted to join in. In 2016, after Uzi's new single, "Money Longer," debuted at Number 92 on the *Billboard* Hot 100, he began selling out shows. In the next year, Uzi performed in almost 100 concerts across the United States.[3]

FLYING HIGH

Uzi became known for his crazy stunts onstage, especially for launching himself off the stage to surf across the crowd. At a concert in December

2017 in his hometown of Philadelphia, Uzi climbed up through the bleachers, followed by burly security guards. He reached the second level and mixed with fans while continuing to perform. He then tucked his diamond-encrusted chains into his sweater, tossed his hat down to the crowd, and launched himself from the railing into the crowd below.

He became a regular at the Rolling Loud concert in Miami, where he was known for his antics. In 2017, he launched himself into the crowd from the stage. In 2018, he climbed up to a perch more than 20 feet (6.1 m) in the air before jumping into the arms of waiting fans.

Uzi is an athletic dancer, often seen in videos break-dancing on the street. In 2018, Uzi was the first major rapper to help make the Dallas-based dance called the Woah go viral. He performed the move in a video with 10k.Caash, who was a well-known local rapper. The Woah consists of rocking back and forth, moving the hands in circular motions, and then freezing in place momentarily.

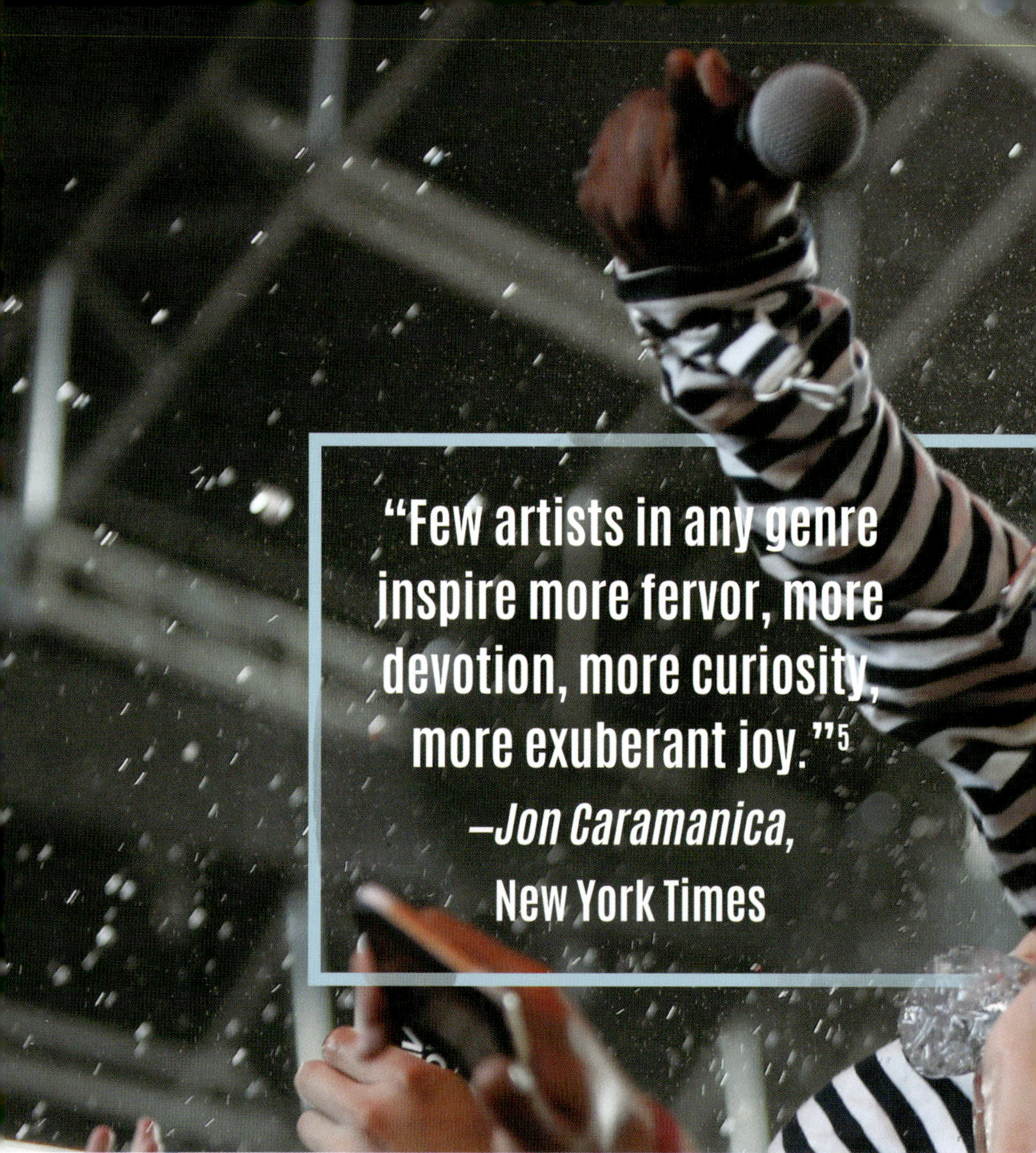

Interaction with fans has become a trademark of Uzi's live performances.

Lil Uzi Vert was a sensation to audiences. He was young and successful. He was a fantastic entertainer. Plus, he enjoyed interacting with his fans and felt it was

important to be genuine with them, even though they
at times chased him down after concerts to get close to
him—in one case forcing him to climb a fence to escape.

FASHION

Lil Uzi Vert became known not only for his unique music but also for his facial tattoos, piercings, and eccentric fashion. His hair has been a kaleidoscope of colors, including red, blue, pink, and purple. He has said that he thinks he does fashion even better than music because for him music is easy, and he puts more effort into looking good.

Shopping is a passion for Uzi, and he shops for clothes in both the men's and women's sections. With his small stature, Uzi can easily fit into women's clothes, and he finds that they often fit better than men's styles. In addition, the women's sections tend to have a much greater variety in style and color than the men's sections.

Uzi has loved clothes since the beginning of his career. He often brags about his clothes on videos, throwing out brand names like Dior, Chanel, Louis Vuitton, Gucci, and Saint Laurent. Uzi buys what he likes—especially since, after his success in the music industry, he has the money to spend. He mixes brilliant colors and crazy patterns,

Like many modern hip-hop stars, Lil Uzi Vert developed an interest in clothing and jewelry.

Supreme
CHICKIE'S &
Famous
CRAB
CHICKIE'S
CHICKIE'S
#ShowUsYour

and he may throw in a matching purse and lots of jewelry. He paid $220,000 for one diamond-studded chain featuring Marilyn Manson wearing Mickey Mouse ears as a tribute to his favorite rock star.[1] He says he doesn't care what anyone thinks about his fashion choices. What's important is what makes him feel right.

"Honestly, in my heart, I think I do this (fashion) better than music. Cause the music s— is effortless. I actually take my time with this."[2]

—Lil Uzi Vert

SHOPPING WITH UZI

A shopping trip with Uzi is frenetic. He dashes through stores and grabs what he wants, not knowing whether it fits. If he changes his mind or it doesn't end up fitting, he just gives it away later. He shops with friends like Kanye West and Virgil Abloh, a fashion designer who has worked with West and is now an artistic director for Louis Vuitton, the French high-end fashion powerhouse. Abloh has been a longtime friend of Uzi's, and they have collaborated on several projects.

After a shopping trip, Uzi's hotel room may resemble an explosion of fabrics, jewelry, and whatever else caught his eye. This may include his favorite junk foods. Uzi is allergic to chocolate, but he likes to stock up on his favorite snacks, including Pop Tarts, mini muffins, and sour candy.

Once Lil Uzi Vert has his ensembles perfected, he often posts fit pics like other fashionistas on Instagram. Fit pics are fashion shots, usually full-length, showcasing an outfit. But Uzi goes a lot further. He may take a full-length shot and then invite viewers to swipe to find the details of each high-end piece of the outfit. Fans often see him in an interview showing off his treasures.

Uzi has also gotten more directly involved in the fashion industry. He was featured in New York fashion designer Thom Browne's Thanksgiving collection in 2019. Uzi was photographed

Uzi has incorporated a wide array of accessories into his fashion, both on and off the stage.

for the campaign playing football while wearing a pleated skirt and a blazer from the collection.

THE DIAMOND IMPLANT

Uzi has had various tattoos and piercings over time, but the diamond implant in his forehead has caused the greatest sensation. He has had a large pink diamond embedded in his forehead above and between his eyes.

KANYE WEST AND FASHION

Successful rappers have long been eager consumers of luxury products. Kanye West is famous for his obsession with fashion. He is known for his sense of style and high-end clothing labels. He has expanded his empire by creating products such as Yeezy shoes, which are produced and sold by Adidas. In 2020, he filed a trademark for Yeezy Beauty, which laid the groundwork for a potential line of makeup, nail polish, perfume, and other beauty products. That same year, West also teamed up with the Gap to produce a new product line.

"Lil Uzi isn't even human. He is another level of a creative being. To me he is an Impressionist painter replacing pigments with ready-made brands and clothes."[3]

—*Virgil Abloh*

The rare pink jewel is reportedly worth around $20 million.

He purchased the diamond in 2017 and made payments for several years before having it implanted. Having a large diamond implanted in your forehead is not an easy procedure. The jewelers put a special mounting of precious metals in Uzi's forehead to lock the jewel in place.

Some speculate that Uzi's diamond is in honor of his love of the anime *Naruto*. The character Tsunade features the Strength of a Hundred Seal, a purple diamond shape on her forehead. It was also great publicity for both himself and the company that implanted it at a time when he was hyping his new projects. Or, as usual with Uzi's fashion choices, the real answer may be simply that he liked it.

UZI'S GARAGE

Once Lil Uzi Vert started making money, he bought his grandmother a house and he bought his first car, a Lamborghini. Since then he has built a collection of custom cars. Together, they are worth millions of dollars.

The car collection is not as large as some people think. Instead of buying new cars, Uzi often has cars reworked with custom colors or colorful wraps. Uzi sometimes chooses to redo his cars with anime characters, such as those from *Cowboy Bebop*. His Lamborghini has gone from military green with black rims to battleship grey with orange rims to a design based on the anime *Mobile*

ANIME

Anime is a style of animation from Japan. It is known for its colorful graphics and action-filled plots. The stories often have fantasy or futuristic themes, but anime includes all types of plots, from romance to comedy. Anime stories are written for all age groups, including children, teens, and adults. Anime gained widespread popularity in the United States in the 1990s. Since that time, movies, TV shows, and merchandise have flooded the US market as a new generation has grown up with anime.

A Bugatti Veyron is sleek, fast, and extraordinarily expensive.

Police Patlabor to flat black. The designs often incorporate the number 16, which represents the block in Philadelphia where Uzi grew up. To match the exteriors, he has custom engine and interior work done.

For his twenty-fifth birthday gift to himself, Uzi spent $1.5 million on a Bugatti Veyron—a car that had been previously owned by boxer Floyd Mayweather Jr. He spent $500,000 on a bulletproof USSV Rhino GX, a type of luxury SUV.[4] Uzi also owns a Rolls-Royce, a Bentley, and others. Uzi's cars are often seen in clips of him with his fans on the streets.

"I just want [the Bugatti], bro! It looks so nice. Like, I'm one of those types of guys. I have to buy *everything*."[5]
—Lil Uzi Vert

P.E.18.
Printemps-Été 20.. Bois de Boulogne
PARIS

IT'S NOT ALL FUN

In his early twenties, Uzi was living his dreams. He was a star with hordes of adoring fans eagerly flocking to his concerts and awaiting his next album. He had the attention of the professional music industry, having been nominated for two Grammy Awards. He had money and a high-end lifestyle. He finally had the attention he had craved as a kid. Still, there were some problems his success and fame couldn't solve.

On June 18, 2018, Uzi's fellow rapper XXXTentacion, born Jahseh Dwayne Onfroy, was shot and killed in Florida. The two rappers had been vying for the top spot on the charts in 2017, with Uzi taking Number 1 for *Luv Is Rage 2* and XXXTentacion taking Number 2 for *17*. This loss hit hard for Uzi, who had just shot to the top with a song about depression and suicide. XXXTentacion was only 20 years old. Uzi launched a foundation for the deceased

Recognition from awards shows, such as the Grammys, showed the professional progress Uzi was making, but personal struggles threatened to derail his career.

XXXTentacion was shot and killed on June 18, 2018. In a video done just before his death, he said, "Worse things comes to worse, I f— die or a tragic death or some s—, and I'm not able to see out my dreams, I at least wanna know that the kids perceived my message and were able to make something of themselves."[1]

rapper's family and child, asking for support from fellow rappers.

Death among rappers of the hip-hop generation was not unusual, and Uzi had been affected by others before. In 2017, Lil Peep, born Gustav Ahr, died by overdose at the age of 21. At that time, Uzi vowed

The 2018 murder of XXXTentacion was a devastating loss for Uzi.

to give up drugs. It wasn't easy. He had been on Xanax, a prescription medication for symptoms of anxiety and panic attacks. Sudden withdrawal from the drug caused shakes. Quitting drugs suddenly can be dangerous, and medical professionals generally warn against doing it. People who want to quit drugs should seek advice on how to do so safely from their doctors. Uzi tweeted about cursing his loved ones and fighting with people at the studio as he went through withdrawal.

FAMILY

In September 2018, Lil Uzi Vert released "New Patek," the first single from the upcoming album *Eternal Atake*. The song is about getting his new piece of bling, an outrageously expensive Patek Phillipe watch. The song got great reviews. Sheldon Pearce wrote for Pitchfork that "Uzi unleashes some of his most cartoonish inventive raps

PATEK PHILIPPE

Patek Philippe & Co. is a luxury Swiss watchmaker founded in 1839. Its watches have become a must-have accessory for ultra-wealthy artists of the new generation, overtaking older brands such as Rolex and Nautilus. One feature that is popular about the Patek is that it is easy to get it customized by a jeweler by adding more diamonds or other bling to the plain face. This makes each of the watches one of a kind—perfect for the individualism of a new generation of artists like Lil Uzi Vert.

As with many rappers, Uzi's lyrics sometimes refer to his latest fashion and luxury purchases.

yet."[2] Charles Holmes in *Rolling Stone* called the six-minute rap "extremely long and extremely good."[3]

Even with the success of "New Patek," toward the end of 2018 Uzi was showing signs of stress. In October he ducked out at the last minute from a concert in Arizona. When he refused to schedule a date for a new concert or reimburse the promoters for their expenses, they sued him for the $600,000 they had lost.[4]

Unknown to the rest of the world, he was having family problems. Uzi was very close to his grandmother. She had given him a place to live when he dropped out of high school. She had encouraged and supported him in his music career. Now Uzi's beloved grandmother had to have a tumor removed from over her eye. She then had a stroke, paralyzing her entire left side. She was in the hospital and then in rehabilitation for months. It was a devastating time for Uzi.

Uzi didn't share his anguish and worry with his fans until his grandmother was finally released from the hospital and rehabilitation on August 22, 2019. That day he finally tweeted about what had happened, saying, "IF YOU DONT KNOW THATS WHO RAISE ME. I love my grandma more than Clothes."[5] He apologized for keeping his fans in the dark, explaining that he just needed some private family time.

FEUDING WITH GENERATION NOW

In addition to his other problems, Uzi had long been feuding with DJ Drama and Don Cannon of Generation Now. He blamed them for the slow release of his work.

He had signed with them in 2015 and released several mixtapes within just a year, but by 2016 he was blaming them for delays in new material. His *Luv Is Rage 2* album had been delayed, and he was venting on social media about the problem. Cannon said that mixing and mastering were holding up the process.

Uzi's team blamed the slow trickle of new releases on delays in the audio production process.

More problems arose between Uzi and DJ Drama in 2018. The precise reasons were not publicly clear, but Uzi vented on social media, warning fellow artists: "If y'all do sign ... sign 2 a major Dont sign 2 a rapper or a DJ."[6] By December, Uzi was plotting to leave Generation Now. He didn't want to work with anyone who tried to change him.

After the release of *Luv Is Rage 2* in 2017, fans patiently waited for a new project from Uzi, but it kept getting delayed. Uzi then blamed the record label because he wanted to release more songs. Don Cannon admitted Uzi made about 700 songs a year, the vast majority of them unreleased.[7] On the other side, Generation Now members claimed they were not holding up his work. Uzi was recording in Philadelphia and not communicating with Generation Now, so they were having trouble planning promotions and a release date for his new album, *Eternal Atake*.

FEUD WITH RICH THE KID

Lil Uzi Vert has had fights—both online and physical—with several other rappers. He once punched rapper Reese La Flare in the face, but he later apologized. Uzi and Playboi Carti also had physical fights, but they eventually worked together. But in 2018, Atlanta rapper Rich the Kid, born Dimitri Leslie Roger, and Lil Uzi Vert got into a high-profile feud after Rich the Kid responded to a tweet from Uzi bashing DJ Drama. Rich the Kid teased that Uzi should have signed with his Rich Forever Music imprint instead of going with the big guys. Uzi responded that he wasn't signing for

"I don't like being famous."[8]
–Lil Uzi Vert

"20racks," meaning $20,000.[9] Two days later, Rich offered Uzi a spot with Rich Forever Music, but by early February he said in an interview that he wouldn't sign Uzi for

Rich the Kid was the subject of one of Uzi's highest-profile feuds yet.

personal reasons. Uzi responded by posting a photo of himself holding a giant crab labeled Rich the Kid.

A day after Rich the Kid's song "Plug Walk" hit platinum, Uzi released "Rich Forever," which featured pointed attacks on his adversary. Rich the Kid then went on Instagram to share lyrics from an upcoming track that included jabs at Uzi, such as "your money gettin' shorter," referring to Uzi's hit "Money Longer."[10] Rich the Kid, who had dyed his hair green, accused Uzi, with his newly dyed green hair, of stealing his look—though Uzi had used the color years before.

The barbs continued until the conflict came to a head in June. Both rappers were in Philadelphia for the Roots Picnic, an annual music festival hosted by the hip-hop group the Roots. Following an earlier exchange of words, they had a physical altercation at a local Starbucks. Someone with Uzi threw a punch at Rich the Kid, who stepped over the Starbucks counter to avoid the attack. No one was hurt.

QUITTING MUSIC

Lil Uzi Vert was under a tremendous amount of stress in both his personal and professional life. His schedule had

been brutal. He was performing at almost 100 concerts a year, plus putting out his own music and collaborating with other artists. He was making millions of dollars, but he was learning that having the money to buy whatever he wanted didn't make him happy. He was starting to feel burned out, so he began neglecting his music. He didn't perform any concerts between December 2018 and April 2019.

In January 2019, Lil Uzi Vert announced he was retiring from music. He said he just wanted to get back to normal. Although buying things like jewelry and clothes did not help with his depression, he found that the one thing that did make him feel good was buying things for his family, such as the house he bought for his grandmother. Uzi started to realize that possessions didn't matter nearly as much as family. When asked what really matters, Uzi responded, "When I go outside and I got a day when no one asks me for a picture. I write those down."[11]

His fans were devastated that the young rapper was retiring. Many people didn't believe it. They thought it was

> "(I'm) flexing so hard and buying the world because deep down I'm hurt."[12]
>
> —Lil Uzi Vert

a stunt to get attention or put pressure on Generation Now to negotiate a better contract. A few months later he released some music on Instagram Live, but it was only old songs from earlier in his career that had not yet been released. Fans were left wondering what would come next for Uzi.

UZI'S BACK

Uzi had begun teasing his second album, *Eternal Atake*, during the summer of 2018. By the end of the year, fans were eagerly awaiting its release. Instead, Uzi had announced his retirement.

On March 20, 2019, the artist NAV announced that Uzi wouldn't be making a guest appearance on his new album, *NAV's Bad Habits*, because Generation Now refused to release Uzi's verse. On March 28, Uzi released the song "Free Uzi" on SoundCloud. "Free Uzi" was his anthem to be liberated to do his own thing. In no uncertain terms, he railed against working with big companies that he felt took unfair advantage of artists. "Free Uzi" was soon removed from streaming services due to copyright issues concerning the right to use the beat in the song.

On March 28, 2019, Uzi signed a deal for management at Roc Nation, a company cofounded by rap legend Jay-Z. Roc Nation tried to negotiate a deal with Generation Now to free Uzi from his original managers. Uzi wanted a greater share of the

When Uzi returned to the public eye, he resumed hyping up his hotly anticipated new album, *Eternal Atake*.

profits from his work, as well as the money Generation Now had promised to cover the cost of studio time and recording. In addition, he wanted more freedom to release whatever he wanted.

Despite his feelings about Generation Now, Uzi missed working in the studio. On March 31, he released the songs "Sanguine Paradise" and "That's a Rack" as negotiations continued. He also did some collaborations. In August, Young Thug released his new album *So Much Fun*, which featured the song "What's the Move" with Lil Uzi Vert.

Although Uzi had shot to the top in the hip-hop world, *Eternal Atake* was only his second album. By 2020, he had been recording for the album for two and a half years. He had begun working at DJ Drama's studio in Atlanta, then moved production to Philadelphia. Kesha Lee,

Young Thug, *left*, had earlier appeared with Uzi at the BET Hip-Hop Awards in 2016.

who had worked as his engineer from the beginning, followed him up there. A huge amount of the work fell to Lee, who said working with Uzi was "creative production engineering."[1] She worked in all aspects of production, from finding beats to recording to mixing, actually living in the studio much of the time.

By the end of 2019, Uzi was again doing promotions for the *Eternal Atake* album. He released the album's first single, "Futsal Shuffle 2020," on December 13. It debuted

"Eternal Means forever. Atake means 2 overtake."[2]
–Lil Uzi Vert in a tweet on July 16, 2018

at Number 5 on the *Billboard* Hot 100, doing even better than "XO Tour Llif3" had done.

"Futsal Shuffle 2020" was released with a catchy video of Uzi and others doing the dance introduced by the song. It even had a slow-motion part where Uzi demonstrated how the dance was done. The fast beat and complicated footwork were a catchy way to introduce his new album. In January 2020, he showed off a new dance called the Glitch. Imitating the motion of a stuck vinyl record, the Glitch requires a jerk each time the foot is tapped. It may have been a tribute

Uzi performed at the Rolling Loud festival in Los Angeles in late 2019.

to the early days of rap, when DJs physically scratched vinyl records.

On March 1, 2020, Uzi released "That Way," the second single from *Eternal Atake*. The song samples the Backstreet Boys' "I Want It That Way." The mixture between 1990s boy band and modern emo rap worked. Fans were going crazy with anticipation as these new songs from the album were released.

A few days later, on March 3, Uzi released a short film called *BabyPluto*, which he helped direct along with

Gibson Hazard. In the film, Uzi plays a mundane office worker who is abducted when an alien spaceship lands on Earth. There is no dialogue, but the colors and effects pull the watcher into the world of *Eternal Atake*. Finally, after all the time and drama, Atlantic released Uzi's long promised album, *Eternal Atake*, on March 6, 2020.

OUT OF THIS WORLD

Eternal Atake is the tale of Uzi's abduction by aliens and travel through space.

The album is divided into three parts that represent different aspects of Uzi. It begins with the introduction of the aggressive character Baby Pluto. The next section introduces the character Renji. Renji represents the rock star side of Uzi's persona. In these songs Uzi wonders whether the wealth and fame of being a star are really keeping him apart from others. Uzi tells the third part as himself, visiting the wonders of the universe as he returns to the real Uzi. Skits between the songs help tell the story. Uzi first created skits with more dialogue that totaled about 20 minutes. Lee liked it but knew they were too long, so she had to cut them dramatically. Ultimately they ended up lasting about ten seconds each.

The album was a sensation. *Eternal Atake* debuted at Number 1 on the *Billboard* 200 and had 400 million streams the first week.[3] Keith Caulfield of *Billboard* thought the success of *Eternal Atake* on online platforms was due to three factors: the long wait for new Lil Uzi Vert

Critics cited the rising popularity of music streaming as one of the factors in *Eternal Atake*'s runaway success.

material, the popularity of streaming, and the fact that the hip-hop genre dominates streaming.

RAVE REVIEWS

Danny Schwartz of *Rolling Stone* called *Eternal Atake* Uzi's best yet, saying that it had a "slick concept and performance that justifies every ounce of hype."[4] The special audio effects, done by Lee, tie the story together. The brief skit of Uzi getting sucked into a portal, along with the sounds from the spaceship and the universe beyond, create a narrative on the album that extends past the songs themselves.

In 2020, *Time* magazine named *Eternal Atake* one of the best new albums of the year. Alphonse Pierre of

Pitchfork said that *Eternal Atake* was "an album that would be chased for years."[6] The *New York Times* called Uzi the "defining rap star of the past few years."[7] The album was nominated for Favorite Rap/Hip-Hop Album at the American Music Awards.

A week after the release of *Eternal Atake*, Uzi released *Eternal Atake: Deluxe: Lil Uzi Vert vs. the World 2*. This version added contributions by rappers Chief Keef, 21 Savage, Future, Young Thug, Gunna, Lil Durk, Young Nudy, and NAV. While the original version had 18 tracks, the deluxe release had 32 tracks. The deluxe version of the album debuted at Number 1, and 22 tracks from it hit the *Billboard* Hot 100 at the same time. Uzi was back.

YOUNG THUG

Young Thug, real name Jeffrey Lamar Williams, was born in 1991. In 2014, he had a breakout collaboration with Rich Homie Quan called "Lifestyle." He created a sensation in 2016 when he wore a blue ruffled dress on the front of his mixtape *Jeffrey*. At that time, rap was known for extreme masculinity. He showed that what someone wore didn't pertain to making great music, and he helped cause a shift from the baggy fashion of hip-hop to more fitted attire. Young Thug created Young Stoner Life Records in 2016. He has helped several young stars get started, including Lil Uzi Vert. Uzi has credited Young Thug for teaching him a lot of life lessons, referring to the fellow rapper as a brother.

Chapter EIGHT

UZI'S NEXT MOVES

Once Lil Uzi Vert was back to work, he kept on dropping more music. In April 2020 he released the single "Sasuke." He had mentioned his love of anime many times, and Sasuke Uchiha was his favorite character from *Naruto*. The ninja Sasuke is on a mission to avenge the Uchiha clan after his brother Itachi killed most of their clan. The release didn't garner nearly the praise of *Eternal Atake*, peaking at Number 65 on the *Billboard* Hot 100.

Uzi kept busy with new collaborations and features. "Multiple Flows" appeared on the deluxe edition of Lil Wayne's album *Funeral*. In June 2020, Uzi joined Alabama artist NoCap on the song "Count a Million." A song about loss and depression, it seemed fitting for the summer of 2020, as the COVID-19 pandemic raged across the world. However, the song didn't get great reviews.

Uzi started 2020 strong, but the COVID-19 pandemic soon prevented the kinds of energetic live concerts he enjoyed.

The characters of Naruto and other popular anime series have spilled over into many areas of pop culture, including the work of Lil Uzi Vert.

LIL WAYNE

Lil Wayne was born Dwayne Michael Carter Jr. in 1982 in New Orleans, Louisiana. He has had a successful career, winning four Grammy Awards in 2009. The rapper has had several brushes with the law for drug possession. He spent eight months at Rikers Island in 2010 for possession of a weapon and wrote the memoir *Gone 'Til November: A Journal of Rikers Island* in 2016. He was arrested again in 2019 for transporting a loaded gun on his private jet and pleaded guilty. He was pardoned by President Donald Trump.

In November 2020, Lil Uzi Vert and Future released a collaborative album called *Pluto x Baby Pluto*. The album hit Number 2 on the *Billboard* 200 chart, and ten songs from the album debuted on the *Billboard* Hot 100 chart. At Number 31, "Drankin N Smokin" was the highest-ranked song. On January 7, 2021, Future and Uzi released a video

for "Drankin N Smokin"
featuring a high-end party
with money, women, and
a hookah.

2020
VIRTUAL CONCERT

Live concerts for 2020
were canceled due to
the ongoing pandemic.
On August 27, Lil Uzi Vert
partnered with Live Nation
to hold a virtual concert.

UZI'S GAME

In addition to making new music, Lil Uzi Vert made other inroads on promoting his brand. There is a playable video game based on his work called *Pluto x Baby Pluto the Game*, which was developed by Krool Toys. The game was a promotion for Future and Lil Uzi Vert's collaborative album. Modeled after games for the Game Boy Color, a handheld console from 1998, it allowed players to control Uzi and fly a spaceship.

A live-streamed show was an experience far different from a live concert and its exciting energy.

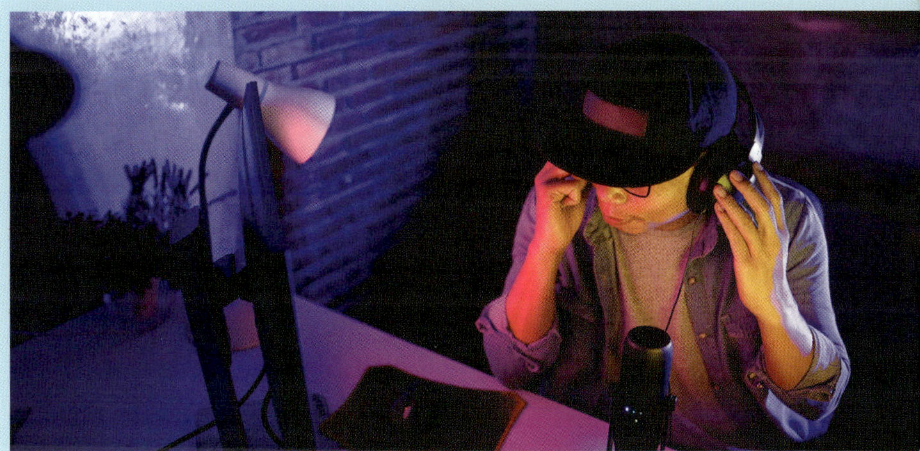

Ticket prices were $15 for the streamed show. Toward the beginning of the event, Uzi told the viewers, "There's a lot going on, but I just want to make sure y'all good."[1]

Alone on a circular stage, Uzi went through many of his most popular songs and performed many of the songs from *Eternal Atake* for the first time. The set flashed with lights and animations. He danced and then ended the concert lying on the stage.

It was a challenge to do a high-energy concert Uzi-style with no audience. Uzi's performances depend on the energy from fans and his interaction with them. Although he performed his heart out, it was no surprise that during the event he said, "I'm not going to keep doing this. If they don't have real shows soon, I'm clearly going to throw my own real show."[2]

TWO NEW ALBUMS

In December 2020 Lil Uzi Vert began dropping songs and interacting with fans on social media. He hinted there were two new projects in the works. They would be called *Luv Is Rage 3* and *Forever Young*.

In March 2021, he did a collaboration with Justin Bieber. The song, "There

Justin Bieber has collaborated with many artists from different genres over the course of a career lasting more than a decade.

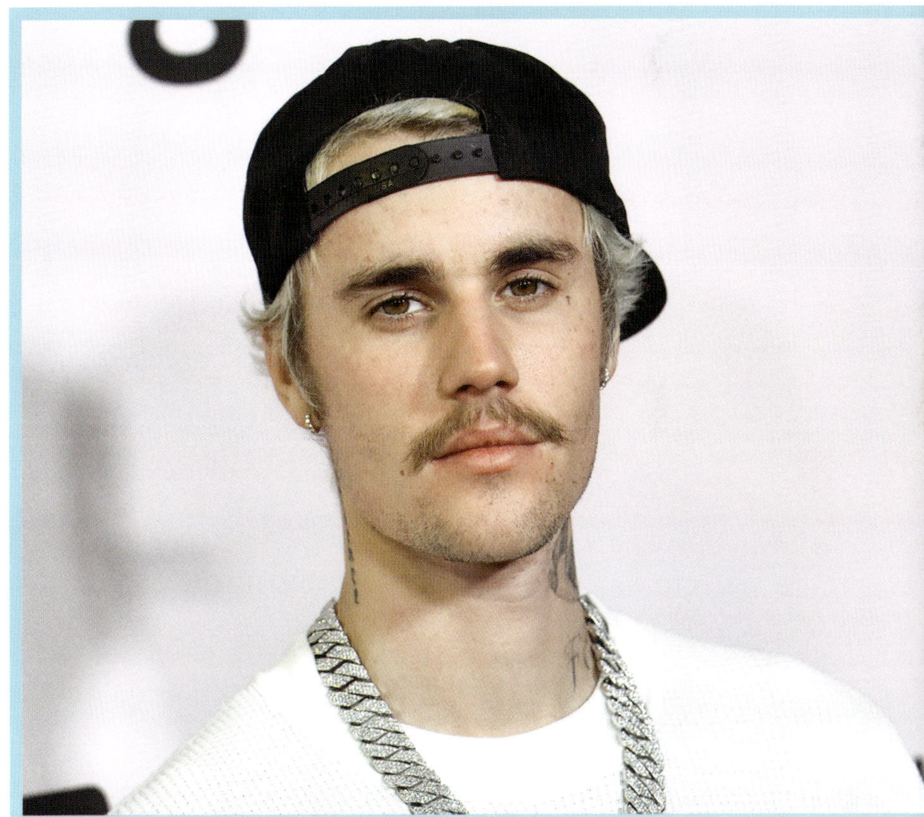

She Go," was on the deluxe edition of Bieber's album *Justice (Triple Chucks Deluxe)*. Bieber predicted the song "would probably be huge on TikTok because it kind of has that feel to it."[4]

While fans awaited Lil Uzi Vert's newest music, Uzi moved deeper into the commercial fashion world. In 2021, he was featured in creative consultant Heron Preston's new collection for Calvin Klein. Multiple stars appeared in the campaign. "But," fashion journalist Max Grobe wrote, "it's Lil Uzi Vert who undeniably understood the assignment, stealing the show in a series of crisp fits."[5]

JUSTIN BIEBER

Justin Bieber was born in 1994 in Stratford, Ontario, Canada. At 12 years old, he came in second place in a local talent show, and Bieber's mother posted some clips on YouTube. Within two years he had a major record deal with superstar singer Usher. He was the first artist to have four singles on the Top 40 before his first album was released. At 25 years old, Bieber became the youngest artist to have seven albums reach the top spot on the *Billboard* Hot 200, breaking the record of Elvis Presley.

INFLUENCE AND IMPACT

Uzi's phenomenal rise in the music business could be attributed to several factors. He was influenced by many genres of music. He listened to acts including Mike Jones, the Ying Yang Twins, and Smash Mouth. He became a huge fan of Marilyn Manson while in high school. He liked the melodies of Hayley Williams of the rock band Paramore.

In the beginning, he was known for his rapid delivery—thus the name Lil Uzi. From the beginning, Uzi had a unique musical quality. His music felt fresh and new. His voice has a nasal quality that others have tried to emulate. At the same time, his rock influence resulted in melodies that differed from what others in the rap world were doing. Music critics use labels to talk about different genres or subgenres of hip-hop. Uzi has moved through a lot of these labels, including rap, trap, emo, and punk

Uzi has combined influences from the past with his own unique artistry to become a major player in modern hip-hop.

RAP STYLES

As new artists become popular, people try to categorize their styles by giving them particular names. There are more than 20 rap genres that people have defined, and Lil Uzi Vert has been placed in several of them, including rap, trap, emo, and mumble rap. Rap is a part of hip-hop that is notable for its rapid, rhythmic recitation of rhyming lyrics over a background beat. Trap is a specific type of rap that is about the drug scene, a trap being a place where drugs are sold. Emo is music that has an emphasis on emotion. Mumble rappers tend to slur words together.

"I feel like he's hit on our platform like no other artist because he's always setting the tone instead of always being a part of something that's going on."[2]

—Lisa Ellis, global head of music, artist relations, and label services at SoundCloud

rock. He has managed to combine these influences into a sound that is his own.

The young Uzi began in a style of rap that he described as a whole bunch of "ayes" and "yeahs" which would then rhyme with anything.[1] The way he creates songs is similarly unconventional. Producer Bugz Ronin described Uzi's recording process as spontaneous. In three of the songs from *Eternal Atake*, "Baby Pluto," "Homecoming," and "Lo Mein," Uzi didn't hear the beat until he was in the recording booth starting his rap. Today, many producers try to emulate Uzi's style of beats, a tribute to his success and influence.

Lil Uzi Vert came into hip-hop in an era when music streaming was beginning to give artists more power over their own work. In an earlier time, only large record companies could coordinate major album releases. They stood between artists and their fans. But with streaming, artists could form more

BUGZ RONIN

Bugz Ronin was born Daniel Perez in 1983 in Stroudsburg, Pennsylvania. He began rapping early and used to play beats during lunchtime rap sessions in high school by banging on a table. He started sending beats to Lil Uzi Vert's manager in 2016, which eventually landed him work producing five of the songs on *Eternal Atake*.

direct connections with listeners. It also allowed artists to experiment with different genres, rather than be forced into a single type of music for commercial reasons. Uzi has taken full advantage of this freedom.

LOVE THE FANS

Besides being a musician, Lil Uzi Vert is a tremendous showman. Like his idol, Marilyn Manson, he became known for his stage performances and eccentric style of dress. He does few formal interviews, which had been a mainstay of music promotion in the old studio era. Instead, he interacts directly with fans on Instagram Live and other social media platforms.

"I like making music, and I like making people happy, but the music is whatever, bro. I really do it just to make my family happy. Like, it's just something for my family to talk about."[3]
—Lil Uzi Vert

Lil Uzi Vert's spontaneity is part of what charms his fans. Internet videos show Uzi as the common person he seeks to be. He interacts with fans walking down the street or at stores or amusement parks. One video shows him jumping off his ATV to talk to some kids on a school bus. He eats a lime Popsicle as he explains that it's only his third day in the area.

Uzi says he lives in the moment. When he records, he is fully into his music. When he is onstage, he is fully with his fans. When he shops, he does so with manic excitement, whether he is buying high-end fashion items or junk food. Uzi always tries to be present, and his fans want to share those exciting moments with him.

NEW VENTURES

Music has made Lil Uzi Vert's fortune, but it may not be enough to contain his creative energy. Jay-Z's Roc Nation has joined Random House Books in a new publishing imprint called Roc Lit 101. Some books from the imprint feature memoirs from entertainment and music stars. Lil Uzi Vert signed a deal

Uzi has become an icon of the streaming and social media age.

to pen an illustrated work of fantasy fiction. Fans began to imagine Uzi's live appearances including book signings in addition to the raucous concerts for which he is best known.

No one could predict what Uzi would do next. He was likely to continue his work in genre-expanding music. His interest in the fashion world suggested

MENTAL HEALTH

Uzi has experienced depression, and the hip-hop community has lost many artists through suicide. Uzi's huge breakout song, "XO Tour Llif3," was about depression, addiction, and suicide. The song eventually reached more than one billion streams. This has made Uzi a voice in helping rappers talk about mental health issues and advocating for mental health.

that he might someday design his own brand. His interest in publishing pointed to a possible future as an author. But fans wondered whether the most likely path would be for Lil Uzi Vert to decide to do something no one had even imagined. As a young man just a few years into his successful career, the possibilities for Uzi's talent and energy felt endless.

"You can't fake real. I think he has punk rock in him. He's a little crazy. . . . He has an attitude like I did and I like that about him."[5]
–*Marilyn Manson about Lil Uzi Vert*

TIMELINE

1994

Lil Uzi Vert is born Symere Woods on July 31 in the Francisville area of Philadelphia, Pennsylvania.

2014

On January 19, Lil Uzi Vert self-releases the mixtape *Purple Thoughtz Vol. 1*. On August 5, he releases the mixtape *The Real Uzi*.

2015

On October 20, Uzi releases the mixtape *Luv Is Rage*.

2016

In April, the mixtape *Lil Uzi Vert vs. the World* and the single "Money Longer" are released.

On July 31, the mixtape *The Perfect LUV Tape* is released.

2017

"Bad and Boujee," a collaboration between Uzi and Migos, reaches Number 1 on the charts.

The song "XO Tour Llif3" is released as a single.

In February, Uzi releases the EP *Luv Is Rage 1.5*.

On August 25, Uzi's first album, *Luv Is Rage 2*, is released.

2018

In September, Uzi releases the single "New Patek."

2019

In January, Lil Uzi Vert announces he is retiring.

Uzi releases the singles "Sanguine Paradise," "Futsal Shuffle 2020," and "Free Uzi."

2020

On March 6, Uzi's second album, *Eternal Atake*, is released.

On March 13, *Lil Uzi Vert vs. the World 2*, a deluxe edition of *Eternal Atake*, is released.

In August, Lil Uzi Vert does a virtual concert during the COVID-19 shutdown.

In November, *Pluto x Baby Pluto*, a collaboration with Future, is released.

2021

The song "There She Go," a collaboration with Justin Bieber, is released in March.

FULL NAME

Symere Bysil Woods

DATE OF BIRTH

July 31, 1994

PLACE OF BIRTH

Philadelphia, Pennsylvania

PARENTS

Unknown; Uzi tends to keep family matters private

EDUCATION

Dropped out of high school at 17 years old

CAREER HIGHLIGHTS

Lil Uzi Vert had his first Number 1 on the charts as a featured artist in "Bad and Boujee" with Migos in 2016. He then gained widespread popularity in 2017 with the song "XO Tour Llif3," which he uploaded to SoundCloud on a whim. His first album, *Luv Is Rage 2*, debuted at Number 1 on the *Billboard* charts in 2017. His second album, *Eternal Atake*, debuted at Number 1 in 2020.

ALBUMS

Luv Is Rage 2 (2017); *Eternal Atake* (2020)

CONTRIBUTION TO HIP-HOP

Lil Uzi Vert's work in the emo rap genre and beyond has expanded the world of hip-hop. His passion for rock artists such as Marilyn Manson have led him to incorporate those influences into his work. Uzi's interest in fashion, and his openness to trying new clothing regardless of the gender it was designed for, have likewise expanded the world of hip-hop fashion. His energetic live performances and direct connection with fans on social media have earned him legions of fans around the globe.

CONFLICTS

Lil Uzi Vert had long-standing conflicts with his recording label, Generation Now. He is extremely prolific in the number of songs he writes, and at times he has become impatient with the slow process of the label releasing his work. He has resisted any attempt to constrain his work to a single genre. He has also had feuds with several other artists, including Rich the Kid.

QUOTE

"I love my songs like my children that I don't have. And once the song is over, it's over. On to the next. It's sad, like, we can't do—I can't make one song forever."

—Lil Uzi Vert

CHARISMA

Charm that inspires devotion in others.

DEBUT

To make a first appearance.

DROP

To release a song or album.

ECCENTRIC

Different or unusual.

EMULATE

To try to equal or excel.

EXTENDED PLAY (EP)

A musical recording of several songs, longer than a single but shorter than an album.

FEUD

An angry, long-lasting quarrel.

FRENETIC

Wild and energetic.

GENRE

A specific type of music, film, or writing.

IMPLANT

Something inserted into the body by surgery.

IMPRINT

A brand with its own name owned by a larger company.

MIXTAPE

A compilation of unreleased tracks, freestyle rap music, and DJ mixes of songs.

NEGOTIATE

To attempt to reach an agreement or compromise through discussion.

SPONTANEOUS

Happening unexpectedly or without an obvious cause.

STREAMING

A way to transmit or receive data, often music, over a computer network, which allows playback to start before all the data is transmitted.

STUNT

An action, often dangerous, done to attract attention.

VENUE

A place where an event, such as a concert, occurs.

SELECTED BIBLIOGRAPHY

Chow, Andrew R., and Cady Lang. "How Lil Uzi Vert Became an Unlikely Superstar of the Streaming Era." *Time*, 26 Mar. 2020, time.com. Accessed 15 June 2021.

"Lil Uzi Vert: 'Luv Is Rage 2' Interview." *YouTube*, uploaded by Apple Music, 25 Aug. 2017, youtube.com. Accessed 15 June 2021.

"The 20 Best Lil Uzi Vert Songs." *Pitchfork*, 27 May 2020, pitchfork.com. Accessed 15 June 2021.

FURTHER READINGS

Chang, Jeff, and Dave "Davey D" Cook. *Can't Stop Won't Stop: A Hip-Hop History (Young Adult Edition)*. Wednesday Books, 2021.

Influential Hip-Hop Artists: Kendrick Lamar, Nicki Minaj and Others. New York Times Educational Publishing, 2018.

Nicks, Erin. *The Weeknd: R&B Megastar*. Abdo, 2022.

ONLINE RESOURCES

To learn more about Lil Uzi Vert, please visit **abdobooklinks.com** or scan this QR code. These links are routinely monitored and updated to provide the most current information available.

MORE INFORMATION

For more information on this subject, contact or visit the following organizations:

TRAP MUSIC MUSEUM
630 Travis St. NW
Atlanta, GA 30318
trapmusicmuseum.us

The Trap Music Museum is an interactive museum that showcases the culture of trap music and provides a platform for new artists. The museum also features an escape room for visitors to experience.

UNIVERSAL HIP HOP MUSEUM
PO Box 6001
Bronx, NY 10451
347-454-2793
info@uhhm.org
uhhm.org

The Universal Hip Hop Museum celebrates and preserves local and global hip-hop music and culture. The museum's collections include a variety of art and artifacts from the history of hip-hop. It offers educational activities and resources for K–12 schools.

CHAPTER 1. ONE DAY

1. Keith Nelson Jr. "DJ PforReal talks Lil Uzi Vert Learning from The Weeknd, Stage-Diving and His New Album." *Revolt*, 23 Apr. 2019, revolt.tv. Accessed 4 Aug. 2021.

2. Nelson, "DJ PforReal."

3. "Lil Uzi Vert: 'Luv is Rage 2' Interview (Apple Music)." *YouTube*, uploaded by Apple Music, 25 Aug. 2017, youtube.com. Accessed 8 Sept. 2021.

4. "Lil Uzi Vert: 'Luv is Rage 2' Interview."

5. Joe Coscarelli. "Have You Heard This Lil Uzi Vert Lyric?" *New York Times*, n.d., nytimes.com. Accessed 4 Aug. 2021.

6. "The 100 Best Songs of 2017." *Pitchfork*, n.d., pitchfork.com. Accessed 4 Aug. 2021.

CHAPTER 2. FAITH

1. "Lil Uzi Vert Links Up with Metro Boomin for 'Wrong.'" *XXL*, 14 Mar. 2016, xxlmag.com. Accessed 5 Aug. 2021.

2. "Lil Uzi Vert Drops 'Lil Uzi Vert Vs. the World' Project." *XXL*, 15 Apr. 2016, xxlmag.com. Accessed 6 Aug. 2021.

CHAPTER 3. THE REAL UZI

1. Darryl Robertson. "The Real Talk of Philly: Lil Uzi Vert's 'Luv Is Rage' Album." *Vibe*, 5 Nov. 2015, vibe.com. Accessed 4 Aug. 2021.

2. Patrick Lyons. "Breakout Artists of 2015." *Hot New Hip Hop*, 11 Dec. 2015, hotnewhiphop.com. Accessed 4 Aug. 2021.

3. "Lil Uzi Vert: 'Luv is Rage 2' Interview (Apple Music)." *YouTube*, uploaded by Apple Music, 25 Aug. 2017, youtube.com. Accessed 8 Sept. 2021.

4. Adelle Platon. "Migos' 'Bad and Boujee' Is the Latest Meme Soundtrack." *Billboard*, 27 Dec. 2016, billboard.com. Accessed 4 Aug. 2021.

5. Dan DeLuca. "Who's Philly's Biggest Rapper? Lil Uzi Vert Set to Headline at Wells Fargo Center This Weekend." *Philadelphia Inquirer*, 6 Dec. 2018, inquirer.com. Accessed 4 Aug. 2021.

6. Raisa Bruner. "Lil Uzi Vert's Post-Grammy Plans Are Extremely Relatable." *Time*, 28 Jan. 2018, time.com. Accessed 4 Aug. 2021.

7. "Lil Uzi Vert: 'Luv is Rage 2' Interview."

CHAPTER 4. FIRST ALBUM

1. Carl Lamarre. "Marilyn Manson Praises Lil Uzi Vert: 'He Has an Attitude Like I Did.'" *Billboard*, 11 Sept. 2017, billboard.com. Accessed 4 Aug. 2021.

2. "DJ Drama & Lil Uzi Vert 'Boys of Zummer Tour' Vlog (WDYW Live)." *OnSmash*, 20 Aug. 2015, onsmash.com. Accessed 4 Aug. 2021.

3. "Lil Uzi Vert's Concert History." *Concert Archives*, n.d., concertarchives.com. Accessed 4 Aug. 2021.

4. Andrew R. Chow and Cady Lang. "How Lil Uzi Vert Became an Unlikely Superstar of the Streaming Era." *Time*, 26 Mar. 2020, time.com. Accessed 4 Aug. 2021.

5. Jon Caramanica. "Lil Uzi Vert, a Hip-Hop Star Beyond Gatekeepers." *New York Times*, 23 Mar. 2020, nytimes.com. Accessed 4 Aug. 2021.

CHAPTER 5. FASHION

1. Carl Lamarre. "Lil Uzi Vert Cops a $220K Marilyn Manson Chain." *Billboard*, 18 Apr. 2021, billboard.com. Accessed 5 Aug. 2021.

2. Samuel Hine. "The Enormous Appetites of Lil Uzi Vert." *GQ*, 18 Sept. 2019, gq.com. Accessed 5 Aug. 2021.

3. Hine, "The Enormous Appetites."

4. "Here's a Look at Lil Uzi Vert's Insane Custom Car Collection." *XXL*, n.d., xxlmag.com. Accessed 5 Aug. 2021.

5. Hine, "The Enormous Appetites."

CHAPTER 6. IT'S NOT ALL FUN

1. "XXXTentacion Has Music with Lil Uzi Vert, The Weeknd and Juice Wrld in the Works." *Hot 97*, 29 Oct. 2020, hot97.com. Accessed 5 Aug. 2021.

2. Sheldon Pearce. "Lil Uzi Vert: 'New Patek.'" *Pitchfork*, 19 Sept. 2018, pitchfork.com. Accessed 5 Aug. 2021.

3. Charles Holmes. "Lil Uzi Vert's 'New Patek' Is Extremely Long and Extremely Good." *Rolling Stone*, 18 Sept. 2018, rollingstone.com. Accessed 5 Aug. 2021.

4. Ben Brasch. "Promoters Sue Atlanta Rapper Lil Uzi Vert for $600K After Canceled Show." *Atlanta Journal-Constitution*, 26 Feb. 2019, ajc.com. Accessed 5 Aug. 2021.

5. @LILUZIVERT. "My grandma been in the hospital for MONTHS man she had a tumor over her eye the Doctors removed half of it when she finally woke she had a stroke on her entire left side and cannot move it. IF YOU DONT KNOW THATS WHO RAISE ME. I love my grandma more than Clothes." *Twitter*, 22 Aug. 2019, 2:39 p.m., twitter.com. Accessed 5 Aug. 2021.

6. @LILUZIVERT. "And if y'all do sign ... sign 2 a major Dont sign 2 a rapper or a Dj .... Its Just Easier When The Time Come For That Fake S—." *Twitter*, 12 Jan. 2018, 2:18 p.m., twitter.com.

7. Eric Skelton. "Don Cannon Says Lil Uzi Vert Makes 700 Songs a Year." *Complex*, 8 Feb. 2018, complex.com. Accessed 5 Aug. 2021.

8. "Lil Uzi Vert: 'Luv is Rage 2' Interview (Apple Music)." *YouTube*, uploaded by Apple Music, 25 Aug. 2017, youtube.com. Accessed 8 Sept. 2021.

9. @LILUZIVERT. "Boy I'm not signing for 20racks." *Twitter*, 12 Jan. 2018, 4:53 p.m., twitter.com.

10. Michael Saponara. "A Timeline of Rich the Kid's Feud with Lil Uzi Vert." *Billboard*, 1 Mar. 2018, billboard.com. Accessed 5 Aug. 2021.

11. "Lil Uzi Vert: 'Luv is Rage 2' Interview."

12. "Lil Uzi Vert Reveals that His Grandmother Suffered a Debilitating Stroke." *Vibe*, 23 Aug. 2019, vibe.com. Accessed 5 Aug. 2021.

13. Samuel Hine. "The Enormous Appetites of Lil Uzi Vert." *GQ*, 18 Sept. 2019, gq.com. Accessed 5 Aug. 2021.

SOURCE NOTES

CHAPTER 7. UZI'S BACK

1. Ben Dandridge-Lemco. "Engineer Kesha Lee on the Long and Demanding Journey to Lil Uzi Vert's 'Eternal Atake.'" *Complex*, 9 Apr. 2020, complex.com. Accessed 5 Aug. 2021.

2. @LILUZIVERT. "Eternal means forever. Atake means 2 overtake." *Twitter*, 16 Jul. 2018, 8:27 p.m., twitter.com.

3. Andrew R. Chow and Cady Lang. "How Lil Uzi Vert Became an Unlikely Superstar of the Streaming Era." *Time*, 26 Mar. 2020, time.com. Accessed 4 Aug. 2021.

4. Danny Schwartz. "Lil Uzi Vert Goes into Interstellar Overdrive on 'Eternal Atake.'" *Rolling Stone*, 10 Mar. 2020, rollingstone.com. Accessed 5 Aug. 2021.

5. Alphonse Pierre. "Lil Uzi Vert: 'Eternal Atake.'" *Pitchfork*, 10 Mar. 2020, pitchfork.com. Accessed 5 Aug. 2021.

6. Pierre, "Lil Uzi Vert: 'Eternal Atake.'"

7. Jon Caramanica. "Lil Uzi Vert, a Hip-Hop Star Beyond Gatekeepers." *New York Times*, 23 Mar. 2020, nytimes.com. Accessed 4 Aug. 2021.

CHAPTER 8. UZI'S NEXT MOVES

1. Carrie Battan. "Megan Thee Stallion, Lil Uzi Vert, and the Emptiness of the Live Virtual Concert." *New Yorker*, 2 Sept. 2020, newyorker.com. Accessed 5 Aug. 2021.

2. Eric Skelton. "Lil Uzi Vert's $15 Virtual Show Was as Weird as He Said It Would Be." *Complex*, 28 Aug. 2020, complex.com. Accessed 5 Aug. 2021.

3. "Lil Uzi Vert: 'Luv is Rage 2' Interview (Apple Music)." *YouTube*, uploaded by Apple Music, 25 Aug. 2017, youtube.com. Accessed 8 Sept. 2021.

4. Hattie Collins. "Justin Bieber ('iPad 7' on Zoom) Reveals the Details Behind His New Album, 'Justice.'" *Vogue*, 19 Mar. 2021, vogue.com. Accessed 5 Aug. 2021.

5. Max Grobe. "Allow Lil Uzi Vert to Show You How to Style Heron Preston X Calvin Klein." *Highsnobiety*, n.d., highsnobiety.com. Accessed 5 Aug. 2021.

CHAPTER 9. INFLUENCE AND IMPACT

1. C. Vernon Coleman. "Lil Uzi Vert and Playboi Carti Talk about What It Means to Be Mumble Rappers." *XXL*, 4 Mar. 2017, xxlmag.com. Accessed 5 Aug. 2021.

2. Charles Holmes. "Lil Uzi Vert Says He Only Makes Music for His Family Now." *Rolling Stone*, 18 Sept. 2019, rollingstone.com. Accessed 5 Aug. 2021.

3. Holmes, "Lil Uzi Vert Says."

4. Carl Lamarre. "Lil Uzi Vert Hit with Community Service for 2016 Dirt Bike Incident: Report." *Billboard*, 30 Nov. 2017, billboard.com. Accessed 5 Aug. 2021.

5. Andrew R. Chow and Cady Lang. "How Lil Uzi Vert Became an Unlikely Superstar of the Streaming Era." *Time*, 26 Mar. 2020, time.com. Accessed 4 Aug. 2021.

INDEX

Abloh, Virgil, 49, 50, 52
anime, 10, 52–53, 81
Aston, William, 15–18
A.Y., 17–18

BabyPluto, 75–76
"Bad and Boujee," 31–33
Bieber, Justin, 85–86
Billboard charts, 7, 11, 27, 31, 38–39, 42, 74, 77, 79, 81, 82, 86
Browne, Thom, 50
Byrd, Brittany, 10

Cannon, Don, 24–26, 28, 35, 61–64
cars, 28, 53–55
COVID-19, 81–84

dancing, 5, 11–13, 42–43, 74–75, 84
Def Jam Recordings, 24–26
diamond implant, 51–53
DJ BuzzWorthy, 23
DJ Diamond Kuts, 23–24
DJ Drama, 26, 28, 40, 61–64, 72
"Do What I Want," 28–29
drugs, 10, 58–59, 82, 90

Eternal Atake, 59, 64, 71–79, 81, 84, 90

fashion, 20, 47–53, 61, 68, 79, 86, 94
feuds, 61–66
"Free Uzi," 71
"Futsal Shuffle 2020," 73–74
Future, 8, 79, 82, 83

Generation Now, 26, 30, 61–64, 69, 71–72
Glitch, the, 74–75
Grammy Awards, 21, 32–33, 39, 57, 82
Gucci Mane, 30–31

Heaven's Gate, 74

Jay-Z, 71–72, 94

Lee, Kesha, 35–38, 40, 72–73, 77–78
Lil Peep, 58
Lil Wayne, 81, 82
#LilUziVertChallenge, 11–13
Luv Is Rage, 26
Luv Is Rage 1.5, 36
Luv Is Rage 2, 11, 26, 35–39, 57, 62–63

Manson, Marilyn, 13, 15, 16, 39, 49, 89, 93, 97
Meek Mill, 16
mental health, 57–59, 68, 81, 95
Migos, 31–33
"Money Longer," 5, 27–28, 42, 66
MTV Video Music Awards, 11, 39

NAV, 71, 79
"New Patek," 59–60

Perfect LUV Tape, The, 28–30
PforReal, 5
Philadelphia, Pennsylvania,
    13, 15–21, 23–26, 28, 42–43,
    54, 64, 66, 72, 76
Pluto x Baby Pluto, 82–83
Prince Paul, 5
Purple Thoughtz Vol. 1, 23

Real Uzi, The, 26
Recording Industry
    Association of America,
    36, 39
Reese La Flare, 64
retirement, 66–69, 71
"Rich Forever," 66
Rich Forever Music, 64–66
Rich the Kid, 64–66
Roc Nation, 71–72, 94
Rolling Loud, 43
Roots Picnic, 66

"Sanguine Paradise," 72, 76
"Sasuke," 81
SoundCloud, 6–8, 18, 23,
    28–29, 71, 90
"Steaktown Anthem," 18, 26
Steaktown Vertical, 17–20

tattoos, 21, 47, 51
10k.Caash, 43
TM88, 7–8

"Uzi," 24

"Way Life Goes, The," 36
Weeknd, The, 5, 10, 37, 84
West, Kanye, 49, 52
"White S—," 23
Williams, Pharrell, 36–37
Woah, the, 43
Working on Dying, 76

"XO Tour Llif3," 8–11, 38, 74
XXXTentacion, 57–58, 84

Young Thug, 26, 72, 79

ABOUT THE AUTHOR

CYNTHIA KENNEDY HENZEL

Cynthia Kennedy Henzel has a bachelor's degree in social studies education and a master's degree in geography. She has worked as a teacher-educator in many countries. Currently, she writes books and develops educational materials for social studies, history, science, and ELL students. She has written more than 100 books for young people.